WHY THE SKY IS FAR AWAY

D1344150

ALSO BY MANDY HAGGITH

Poetry
letting light in (2005)
Castings (2008)
A-B-Tree (2015)

Anthologies
Into the Forest (Saraband, 2013)

Non-fiction
Paper Trails (Virgin Books, 2008)

Novels
The Last Bear (Two Ravens Press, 2008)
Bear Witness (Saraband, 2013)
The Walrus Mutterer (Saraband, 2018)
The Amber Seeker (Saraband, 2019)

Why the Sky is Far Away

Mandy Haggith

POEMS

Mandy Haggith

RED SQUIRREL PRESS

First published in 2019 by Red Squirrel Press
36 Elphinstone Crescent
Biggar
ML12 6GU
www.redsquirrelpress.com

Edited by Elizabeth Rimmer

Typesetting and design by Gerry Cambridge
e: gerry.cambridge@btinternet.com

Cover photograph: Tom Whitfield/Shutterstock

Copyright © Mandy Haggith 2019

The right of Mandy Haggith to be identified as the author
of this work has been asserted by her in accordance with Section 77
of the Copyright, Designs and Patents Act 1988.
All rights reserved.

A CIP catalogue record is available from the British Library.

ISBN: 978 1 910437 80 3

Red Squirrel Press is committed to a sustainable future. This book
is printed in the UK by Imprint Digital using Forest Stewardship
Council certified paper.
www.digital.imprint.co.uk

For Zazzy

Contents

Skinny Dipping * 9
Grandmother Spider * 10
Why the Sky is Far Away * 11
Why we need birds * 13
Gran * 14
The Aunt I Never Met * 15
My Sister's Bedroom * 16
Walking the Bear * 17
Zi Gong * 18
Forty * 19
Paper Daughter * 20
Carry Carry Life Finish * 21
Our Father * 23
Spider * 24
Alphabet * 25
Tweed * 33
Breaking the Silence * 34
Craic * 35
Dubh * 36
A Tree Hug for Bill * 37
Bowline on the Bight * 38
Heartbeats * 39
Dreamcoat * 40
Cave * 41
Not One for Mountaintops * 42
Salinity * 43
Six Takes on Writing * 44
Spreading the Word * 48
The Makar's Bucket * 49
Layby * 50
This is No Place for a Bear * 51
Brown Bear * 52

Bear * 53
Winter Bear * 54
Hyena * 56
Dog * 57
Cow * 58
Seal * 59
Midges * 60
Knowledge * 61
Sundarbans * 62
Bandhavgarh * 64
Fences * 65
I Have My Yellow Boots On to Walk * 66
Under the Surface * 67
Walking * 68
Boats on the Kelvin * 69
The Falkland Burn * 70
Start at the Top * 71
Cutting Peats * 72
Take it Easy * 74
Attune * 75
Green Bowl * 76
Touch the Earth Gently * 77

Acknowledgements * 78
A NOTE ON THE TYPES * 80

Skinny Dipping

I love the wait before the dive:
the build-up, sun on skin, poised

yet teased
by that licking chill of breeze.

I watch what lurks and bites
in grave black water.

I fear I'll freeze.

I touch it with my toes.

Deep breath—
here goes.

Grandmother Spider

from a Hopi creation story

She sat in the glow of the purple dawn light
and sang out this song

> run a line to the east
> where the sun god will rise
>
> pull the line to the west
> where the sun god will sleep
>
> reach the line to the north
> where the great bear will dance
>
> draw the line to the south
> where the hunter will creep
>
> now bring me some clay from the hollow
> red black yellow and white
>
> let's weave all the people and link them together
> and bask in the glow of this purple dawn light
>
> now wrap them in cloud fleece
> and sing them to life

and she sang
and they breathed

and they smiled
in the glow of the purple dawn light

Why the sky is far away

From a story of the Bini people, Nigeria

We used to eat nothing but sky.
It was crisp, delicious, nourishing.
We gorged and grew fat.

When we took more than we needed
and threw waste on the midden
we noticed the sky become bitter.

It was I that took the final slice.
I had quarrelled with my husband,
took my hurt out swiping wildly with my knife.

A piece of sky as big as the roof fell down.
I ate until I felt sick and guilty.
So did he.

We took left-overs to the neighbours
but everyone had plenty, more,
and a rotting heap behind their back door.

I nibbled all night, but by morning
it was fermenting, sticky with flies.
My husband slopped it onto the stinking pile.

When dawn broke
the sky was a mile high fury
and the air was thin, inedible.

Hungry, my husband took to killing animals,
even birds,
and eating their flesh.

I left him and grew thin.
I climb into tree-tops,
eat only fruit from the highest branches.

Why We Need Birds

Owl calls stitch the night,
mending holes made by the moon.

Geese haul clouds,
beating out dust.

Buzzards, lifting the sky,
make space so all the rest of us can fly.

Gran

Wool around, hook in,
tugs out a skein of thoughts of you,
wool around, hook back through.

Fingering the brown wound yarn
I think you would not like this wool,
you'd call it dingy, dull

but I love its tinge of mauve
its faint memory of your
cardigans and slippers.

I'll crochet this for you
despite its muddy shade.
It is woody, earthy

and it smells so soft,
just like your cupboards
with their hoarded hidden colours.

This ball is all my holidays with you
guiding my little fingers,
yours, arthritis-gnarled.

Wool around, hook in; it's so much easier
than I remember, now, missing you,
wool around, hook back through.

The Aunt I Never Met

after Matthew Sweeney

She was the one who didn't go
to Sunday School. The one who skipped
and swam but never sewed or read.
She used to run away with boys
to hide, and when she died
they said she'd loved ten men.
She travelled to the Indies and
to ports of spice and wine.
She wrote a letter to my father
once. It made him smile, then burn.
                    Once in a while
she used to feature on the evening news.
I don't remember why. Do you?
Was it those electric eyes or the clothes
she wore, the baggy dresses like the ones
next door, the flowers in her hair,
that stare? I don't recall.

My Sister's Bedroom

I used to think about your bedroom,
the one the man in the farmhouse
is keeping for you, its pillow waiting.

The draught is cold in winter
through the open window. The view
you would have woken to each morning
is white, trees bowed, hills barren.

He sits by his too big kitchen table, wishing
for a change in the weather, listening
for the sound of your car coming gently
to a crunching halt on the gravel drive
he built last summer for your arrival.

Walking the Bear

I could never keep up with her
when she was walking the bear.
Panting along behind
I would just have to watch them go.

They wove among crowds and traffic
as if stepping between trees
in the forest. Blending in,
camouflaged somehow.

I would catch a glimpse of them
now and again, turning a corner,
crossing a road, but otherwise
they merged into the urban flow.

I guess most people took the bear
for a big brown shaggy dog.
Even I did sometimes. But then
she'd turn her head and you'd know.

Zi Gong

For thirty years the palace has lain empty
awaiting occupation by the empress.
Its corniced corridors are voids, its rooms
have never chimed with a child's play.
No little royal feet have ever stamped here.

Each month the crippled servants
gather with buckets of tears to bleach and scrub.
We drag all the tattered furniture outside
and we wheedle open the sky lights
to let the moon and stars bleed in

hoping the night will bathe everything clean
ready for the coming of the unborn queen.

Forty

not suckling.
not feeding a baby on milk from within.
not having breasts round with nourishment.

not having a life growing inside.
not growing fat in loose dresses.
not watching the belly swell.

not feeling the pain of labour.
not having contractions, pushing, breathing until the waters break.
not being reassured by a midwife.

not smelling the newborn, not hearing its cry.
not smiling at the first yawn, at little fists.
not looking into newly opened eyes.

It's not one of these things.
None of them.
None of them at all.

Paper Daughter

Gestate inside a private room
the person of your choosing. Cut her gently
out of paper, follow dotted lines,
bend along the creases saying, "fold here".

Snip scissors, careful not to crop off curls,
draw in the face you want to set free
smiling, frowning, choose whose eyes
will weep and watch and see.

Press out some clothes to dress her up in,
cardboard jeans and shirt or tissue dress,
hook their paper tabs around her shoulders
sure not to crush their smooth white newness.

Prop her on her stand beside a candle flame.
Feel inside you rustling cells embroider.
Let them replicate as you create
then burn your paper daughter.

carry carry life finish

alone it's hard to hoist
a back-basket full of seaweed

to straighten knees and lift
the woven willow shoulder-borne

the strap across the forehead
padded with soft remnants of a puppet

its comforting tug across the brow
with every footfall

heavier than normal
stepping back in time

remembering a Nepali friend
resting with a doko full of dung

sighing *carry carry life finish*
with a smiling wobble of the head

now it's the slow heave up the hill
the awkward manoeuvre at the gate

hands grasping the knotted rope
grasping the hands of other women

in other countries
in other millennia

marching alone in solidarity
with all the other creel-bearers

singing *carry carry* life finish
though clearly life goes on

Our Father

Our father
who art in the garden
John William be thy name.
Now springtime comes
thy weeding needs done
on earth
as this is our heaven.
Give us this May
a dahlia bed
and grow us a cress patch
as we forgive birds
that pull up the onion sets.
Seed in pots for germination
and deliver us from weevils.
For fine is the springtime
the showers
and the morning glory
for ever and ever,
Cyclamen.

Spider

The spider rushes to a struggling fly
and winds it up
as my mother winds the ball of wool
that rolls off her knee
when I drop
him
into the conversation.

Alphabet

after Inger Christensen

Affirmation

Ash trees are therefore life is.

Beginning

Birches, bracken, brambles and birds,
a bourach, a beautiful bourach.

Continuation

At the coast, a rock-sea confusion.
Crows cruise, caw, congregate on a corpse.
Corrupting carbohydrates become compost.

Death

Dandelions are, dunnocks are, Dad is.
I feel down. I don't do. I doubt.
Duties are doubled.
But dandelions are, and daffodils definitely are too.

Elegy

Evening comes.
Everything exists.
Everything nothing.
Everything exists.
Evening comes.

Fire

I find fire,
flames, fog, finches, frogs and friends.
Looking at the future,
fear, fruit, fiction and freedom
flourish,
fortunes do not.

Grave

good
grey
ground
silence
good
grey
ground

Happiness

You would want us not to grieve too long
so I go to the old hazel tree and lie down
here and now where you are no longer.
You taught me never to hate anyone
no matter how horrible they seem.
We have choices, all life long, until the end.
My hormones are changing, hot flushes happen.
The hazel catkins open tiny yellow flowers.

Imagination

An ivory carving
conjures the iron age
into the present.
Indigo sky:

instant tempest.
Inside others
intractable secrets.
The inner workings of a mind
make the impossible possible.

Justice

Better than a joke
seeing a wrong righted.
Take money from the rich
give it to the poor.
Is it so difficult?
Just listen.
Stop and help.
Gang up together
against the powerful, for good.
Jam tomorrow.

Killing

Does the kingfisher
give itself up to the hawk?
Is kelp
thrown up onto the beach,
clinging with its holdfast to a stone,
murdered by the sea?
Is my omelette
haunted
by unborn feathers and clucking?
Frosted frogspawn on the pond.
Bones along the shore.

Lots

Lots of letters.
Lots of lilies and daffodils.
Lots of leaves.
Lots of liverworts and mosses.
Lots of lovely lichens.
Lots of little animals: woodlice, earwigs, beetles.
Lots of lions: cats, statues and flags.
Lots of lying around.
Lots of lying for your life.
Lots of life.
Lots of loose ends.
Lots of love.

Mum

mourning
my
mother
means
missing
maternal
messages

months
minus
mum

memories
must
make-do

Now

The day he had to leave
I sat with my brother by Mum's bedside, crying.
'Go back to your little family,' she said,
'they need you.'

We talked about the nursery trees
in the Pacific Rainforest, where he lives,
great cedars that live a thousand years,
stand dead five hundred more
then fall, to feed another generation.

They give their nitrogen, nutrients, nature.
Even as only a long, low mound in the woods
the mother tree gives everything
to nourish her offspring.

Only

As there is no omniscient being,
no omnipotent force,
we must be optimistic
as we go from our origins
to oblivion,
from the open-mouthed yowl
to our obituary,
on the way, enjoying
owls in osiers
ogres on oboes
onomatopoeia
occasional orneriness or obduracy
and, obviously, oranges, often.

Primroses

Primroses form patches in woods.
Primrose leaves poke through leaf litter.
Primroses photosynthesise.
Primroses are peaceful.
Primrose petals are so delicate
                    so pale
                    so pretty.
Primrose flowers are pin or thrum—gender balanced.
Primroses are politically correct.
Primroses withstand perishing spring weather.
Primroses point the way to perfection.

Qs

Quietly I grieve.
Quickly I write
questioning everything.
Quietly spring comes.
Quickly bracken unfurls
questioning nothing.
Quietly we die.
Quickly we forget
questioning everything.
How quick we are to question quietness.

Rest

Resting on water
I realise
recreation is possible.

I remember
a red coat
red lips.

Roots grow slowly
reaching inexorably
into rock.

Spring

Between squalls
the sun sometimes
shrugs, shuffles in,
soothing.

Sepals unsheathe,
shoots stretch.
Soon, soon,
a green sheen.

Time

trip plans
travel schedules
table of departures
terrorist clock
tormentor
tomorrow, petty pace
tribulation

Under

A woven coffin
carried by six
strong people,
living, crying.
We have put daffodils
into the earth.

Vim

After primroses come violets.
After wind comes velocity.
After wheels come vehicles.
After conviction comes vehemence.
After patience comes virtue.

Wonder

Wild wet wind in the wiggly woods.
A beetle's sunset-oil-sheen.
A fern unfurling.
A welter of questions about the world.

X-ray

A clot blocking one lung.
Advanced cancer.
No choice but exit.

Yes

You are young yet, she said, live on.
So: yeast, yacht and yellow flowers.

Zone

We go from zoology to zenith to zero.

Tweed

Its rough, red-flecked, silk-lined softness
hangs only in memory. I cannot try it on.

She offered it to me once. My sister too.
Ever tidy, she must have put it to a sale.

So now, although I hunger to shrug it over my shoulders,
put my hands into her pockets, maybe find a 20p,

a tissue to touch or a hankie to hold onto,
there's only a wardrobe to empty

and then a train to catch
back north over the border river

to where that soft-rough fabric came from,
where the big round buttons belong.

Breaking the Silence

'A hovering of wings in mist
Breaks the silence of the eyes
... The sun dries up the tears'
—Lindoro of the Desert by Giuseppe Ungaretti

You wept when we brought you home from hospital.
Tears you couldn't show a doctor
you shared with me, and although you hurt
and that hurt me, the wetness on my hand
felt like a gift, soft as forest moss.
We can only love the ones we love
and all we can do for them is love them.

I have a friend who weeps
whenever someone is kind to him.
He is so thirsty for our love
he has spent his life half-wilted.
There, I say, propping him up in a puddle,
drink. Now go to a pond, soak yourself,
like celery, discover you can stand tall.

I no longer cry. I leave it to those who need the rain.
I inhabit a swamp of plump sphagnum,
sturdy lichens and bog bean blossoms like frilly knickers.
Weep on my shoulder, soldier,
and put down your weapon.
Here is a sundew, look, and the butterworts
will soon be coming into flower.

Craic

he says be quiet
but he doesn't mean it

he means rewind
he means talk forward fast

no need for meanings he says
just look at that—

seals on the skerry
ravens on the crag

a diver flies over
rakrakrakrakrakrakrak

now we're cooking on gas he says
now we're cooking on gas

Dubh

It starts solid as earth beneath stars
when the moon is new.   It ends
quiet as the loch where ravens flew.
Dubh.   Its heart is the skerry mew
of a winter curlew while I'm curled
up under down with you.   Dubh.

A Tree Hug for Bill

I touch the bark
thinking of the texture of your voice,
look up through leaves to sky
remembering your eyes,
feel my thighs, hips, shoulders
press the calmness
in the heartwood of this tree.

I am learning to love you at a distance,
asking birds to cross the sky,
to stitch with their wings the rent we tore,
to gather the folds of hanging air,
repair.

I hold the tree.
I offer it all the longing it will take from me.

Bowline on the Bight

With this special knot he created a loop
that will untie easily when we want it to
but otherwise will hold strong.

By winding the ends around stones,
tossing them over two high branches
and tugging them tight, tight,

tighter than taut,
he suspended the bowline
between these magnificent beeches.

Through the loop he threaded a second string
from which our bag hangs, clasped,
keeping everything safe,

higher than bears can reach.
It's his best piece of string.
This bight must be unbreachable.

Heartbeats

catch a clarsach melody
    a sentimental tug of strings
        across the birches of an evening
            someone else's happy hour
                as everybody's sun sets

hear the birds
    the terns' discordant jazz
        two divers heading home
            a thrush's couplets
                (thrush's couplets)

listen to the wind's song
    rain drums going strong
        with ocean bass
            wild and improvised
                re-inventing freshness

but wake to curlews in the morning
    mewing winter in
        the duvet tight around our eyebrows
            noses warm
                that rhythm in our chests

and know that this, here, now
    this breath
        these hearts are
            where all harmony is grounded
                here all music comes to rest

Dreamcoat

All our lives' fabrics
        woven together,
                entangled, fused.

All of our wishes: passionate reds,
        homecoming yellows,
                hopeful sky blues.

Grey for the clouds
        and their children
                lochans, puddles and streams;

for their mother,
        the ocean,
                apple-sea-green.

Peach for the sunrise,
        pink for its setting
                and white gold for noon.

Silver for spirit,
        for the moment we know
                one with the stars and the moon.

Brown for the earth
        black for the long nights of love,
                love—

all of the colours for love.

Cave

here beyond light
the underground river pulses and pools

troglodyte fish hide under pebbles
beads of moisture linger in cracks

our stone-age feet understand this place
the smell of stalactites hangs

a drip on my cheek
tastes of rock-sprung exhilaration

our laughter splashes into the black
you reach hands out to my voice

and we kiss
enchanted by blindness

Not One for Mountaintops

I grew up in a shadow under the hedge,
love nowhere better than
deep, dense forest.

I've always adored that moment
when the train plunges
into the tunnel.

It's about extinguishing the world—
      under the duvet
        the cupboard under the stair
        the gap behind the sofa
        under-table burrows
—all so much safer than out there.

For years, smiling, trilling, 'I see',
while in my head a voice adds
'said the blind man'.

Now, my hand in front of my face,
to no effect.
Uncompromising blackness.

At home
in the absolute darkness
of the cave

I can see nothing:
at last I know what it is
to be truly delighted.

Salinity

I want to reassure him
that the onset of salinity
need not concern an old seadog like him.

Take the ocean, so much older than the hills
yet still nosing up the shore
and dancing back, twice daily.

We're all a little saline if you ask my view,
what with global warming, sweating's on the rise
and everyone has salt-tears when depressions hit.

If he does it right, he'll start a trend—
forget the 'senior moments', any seasoned sailor
worth his salt must feel a little brackish.

Six Takes on Writing

(1) Lengths

pause

above the still pool
peel off your clothes
and dive

feel the shock of contact
as the splash subsides
then swim

crawling up the lanes
between the pale blue lines
now flow

remember to breathe in and out
each stroke of thought
unwind

enjoy the weightless meditation
aim for perfect even rhythm: thrust
and glide

(2) Seedlings

Keep them moist.
Gentle them.
Some wilt.
Others succumb to frost.
Bring on the rest
but not too quickly.

Pot up.
Give space.
Nip out lush growth.
Show care.

Then harden them off
for the cold world out there.
Ready them
for wrath and wonder.

(3) Tell me a word I do not know

a simple word like rhone
so I can shimmy up

to blag some bree
from a spaewife's stoup

or burgle a new idea or three
then loup

off down a dark back loan

(4) Malus sieversii

My apple began as a bud opened petals
white as forgetting, pink as new dawns.

It is red-skinned like snow white's.
Calvino says the old folk-tales are true. I believe that too.

A bee came to its honey-smell-summons
humming her foraging song

praising the sweetness of works-in-progress
grazing all the ideas of apples, encouraging them.

Rain stores memories underground.
Sunshine makes them flesh.

Later I will prune the tree. But now I wait.
Fruit takes time to form.

(5) Kindling

Some won't go—burn them whole.
But when one does, when the axe hits,

meets no resistance and the log splits,
when it tumbles into two, that's when you know

you have work you can do, then, then,
as the axe falls through,

as the wood falls away and the resin scents
with the scent of everyday, then, then,

for a moment you can see
how a life's fire can begin to be.

(6) Bengali

The moon scribes a laborious ode, letter by letter, in ancient regular form.
Her reflection in the river improvises a Bangla song.

An epic is etched across the mud in a cuneiform of footprints.
Mangrove trees tell forest sagas in runes and ogham.

Long lines are scribbled by rivulets, punctuated by pugmarks.
An alphabet of ducks drafts overhead.

An egret is semaphoring on the river bank.
The current responds with a swirling script of leaves.

My pencil adds a few leaden letters
but the real writing is out there beyond this poem.

Spreading the Word

Yesterday a man approached me in the Dornoch Inn
interrupting my macaroni cheese and wine

saying he'd overheard a comment about poems
and was I 'the Assynt poet' and if so

—what was the Balinese word I'd used
for being in this moment, full of gratitude?

Rahayu, I beamed. He nodded, rahayu.
Smiling, in unison, rahayu.

The Makar's Bucket

for Liz Lochhead, Scotland's new Makar, 2011

Here comes that Glasgow poet
filling her bucket at the stream again.
You know its source is a wild land rock
that swells with rain,
gathers, sweetens, holds

then lets it go
to chuckle and dance, burble and joke,
gush, roar, contemplate, console.

If you've a thirst
this woman will quench it.
She knows where the flow is fresh.
She wants us all to taste at least a drop.

The water of life's in the Makar's bucket.
Take her your beakers,
bring her your cups,
fill them, raise them, sup!

Lay-by

a small brown bundle
lit up in the full-beam headlights
lying exactly where it fell

all the longing
you have realised you felt
since you dropped it

all the loss
you have rehearsed
while seeking

in the woodland
in the glen
and in the other lay-by,

the wrong lay-by,
where your future
was not stretched out in anticipation

the past was merely
empty
with regret,

all that longing and loss, all that love
floods miraculously
into this floppy amber symbol of survival,

all of life left to be lived
defying time, is here
laid-by, illuminated, lifted.

This is No Place for a Bear

it's the back end of Glaswegian amusement
where East Riderz Pay No Poll Tax
and pleasure seekers only come for sleaze

smell the sweet lemon tang of cheap perfume
the people's piss the cigarettes the fastfood trash
one short high mini-skirted moment's bliss

hold nudge hold nudge hold nudge roll
Afghani black or Egyptian gold
it's a cashpot it's an air vent it's scaffold

beware bear beware the night-time shadow watchers
sharp edges in doorways dog shit on kerbstones
there's no food here just plantain buddleia a withered thistle

the old rag-and-bone man says there's too much art here
look: rusty screws broken bottles peeling pin-ups
blocked-in windows street lamps wires

get lost bear go north get out of the freak show
it's a burst balloon it's a skip load of guttering
watch your paws keep out of the bins mind how you go now

go now

Brown Bear

You see me, don't you, when you lift your snout?
Teddy ears like radar dishes swivel.
I am in your range, I see you register.
Our eyes lock on, I gaze, you monitor.

So when you sniff, then drop your head, relax,
a shoot tip here, a whole leaf tongueful there,
I know the grace of being seen, accepted
watcher, neither enemy nor friend.

It's smell that ruins our detente,
dissolving as you catch a whiff of me or mate.
Distaste sends you scampering up the bank.
Our brief truce broken by my human scent.

Bear

'This animal body... remains the primary
instrument of all our knowing.'

—David Abrams

I am camping in an orange tent.
The bear is wild in the forest.

I am 40 years and 5 days old.
The bear is 4.

I have just washed my hair with shampoo.
The bear is in the stream.

I have good quality walking boots that scrunch on the path.
The bear has big furry paws.

I speak conversational French and no Romanian at all.
The bear is quiet.

I sometimes play the piano.
The bear doesn't care.

I am.
So is the bear.

Winter Bear

after Ted Hughes

In a cave among bouldery scree
the bear is sleeping.
She is dreaming fire
inside a rock hollow
shaped like a skull.
The fuel of the fire is bones.

Little, brittle bones of bird people
are giving out flames like songs,
tiny flickering voices of sunshine.
A pelvis bellows with the burn of sex,
femurs shout out in pain.
A pig's trotter grunts and chars.

Sparks chitter from eye sockets
and teeth whisper into ashes.
Two spines, one of an otter, one of a fox,
smoulder in parallel, crumbling,
vertebra by vertebra,
into silence.

The bear sighs in her sleep
soothed by the heat.
Inside her a foetus grows.
In spring the cub will waken
to buds and blossom.
The earth will be hungry again.

But for now, in the dream-flames
hunger is forgotten.
Winter chews on its memories
and smoke trickles
over the twitching nostrils
of the sleeping bear.

Hyena

for John Burnside

I met you, Dog Breath,
panting into my tent
by the black
oozing
crocodile river.

From time to time
I catch a whiff;
your leathery sweat stench
lurks
with memory's foxes.

Your hot breath on my eyelids
jerks me awake
gasping
in tree-creak starlight.
You are still here

gnawing under your acacia
my slavered sandal in your paws,
your ember eyes
creaturely and wise
laughing in my face

delighted by your prize.

Dog

I want to go to the forest but spirits would try to bewitch me. I need a
guide. Luckily, one afternoon, a white dog with black face and a dark
ring on his tail befriends me and leads off south towards the woods.
Scrunching among mixed-age pines, the dog shows where the snow is
least deep, padding along ahead, stitching a route through the drifts.

It is quiet, with just an occasional hum of a distant motorbike and side-
car on the frozen surface of the water, a flock of great tits chattering past,
a crow. The leaves freeze-dried in autumn: the air smells faintly of hay.

The day is warm enough to sit in the sun, absorbing details: crisp, white,
thorny bushes; blond herbs; the tracks of deer; weasel-marks leading to a
hole under a tree; a delicate

    ,,))))

          imprint of a ptarmigan's wing.

The dog sniffs for mice under bushes, nose deep in snow, waiting.

Cow

Are you shy with everyone
or is there a woman who milks you
whom you trust?

I pull long grass from beyond your fence.
You are hungry enough to want it
and approach, belly swinging,
your ears, black, hairy, distrustful.

You snort and reach, neck stretching
for my handful of green.
Your big pink tongue elongates,
curls around the stems, clutches,

then, chewing,
you scatter some
in your haste to get away.
You still don't trust me.

With your cautious brown eyes
you show me my desire to be loved.
I like you for that doubt.
We humans are not, in general, trustworthy.

Seal

big fat seal shining on the seaweed
tossing bladderwrack
galumphing and humping his blubber
wobbling his tail
flipper-flapping himself to get comfy
now with his tiny webbed arm-stump
waving

and I wave back
acknowledging the passing season
the changes in residents

the arrival of water-skiers
the terns' departure for their winter homes
the problem of heron-housing in a time of wind-throw
the absence of cormorant today

it is good to greet
be at least on nodding terms
I live here too
among the thrift, the ripples and the rock-wrack

Midges

a column of dancing midges
whines
like a single mosquito

looking up
each swarm member is bodiless movement
etch-a-sketching on the sky

two land
stand
one 12-legged trestle table

we know so little of the world
its grey smudges
its inscrutable stillness

Knowledge

A gull soars
in azure air over satin sea
out beyond anchors and moorings.

It must know what it is like
to penetrate the blue
rest on a surface of sky
see beyond and through.

So too
crabs burying into mud at loch bottom
badgers among wildwood boulders
tits in tree top interstices
bats in snags
spiders in cracks between window and frame
microbes under the fabrics of our lives

all know places beyond our senses,
all those other places,
all those little vastnesses.

Sundarbans

(1)

If we had seen a tiger
would we have thrilled to
'Crocodile! Crocodile! Crocodile!'?
Would we have known
the mystery of Irrawaddy dolphins,
grace of eagles, falcons, ospreys,
secrets of monitors, boar and deer?

If we had seen the royal cat
would we have appreciated
the regal bearing of adjutants
the kingfisher's iridescent blue?
A tiger is not pure egret white.

A tiger may have interrupted
the perfect symmetry of chevroned banks.
It may have tarnished
the peace of mangrove, mud bank, creek,
the slow tidal ebb and seep,
or broken the silence
welling up when the engine's putt-putt's cut.

If we had seen a tiger
would we have looked so lovingly
or watched so well?
Would we have learned to trust in Bon Bibi
whose forest grows legs and dances,
sinks and swims?
Could we have relinquished the wish,
come simply

to be
in this liminal place

if we had seen a tiger?

(2)

I try to find enlightenment
under the banyan tree
but discover only
six old tyres hanging inside its trunk,
an electric flex
and four empty booze bottles.

Roots nudge apart a brick wall
promising to crumble it,
lay it to dust under fallen leaves.
Bee nests hang
from upper branches,
humming.

I ponder tyres, flex, bottles,
muse on links
between motion, power and spirit.
I am not sure whether,
like a mountain summit,
nirvana can be reached by uphill struggle

or whether, like this tree,
it is a gradual becoming.
Either way, I will heed its guidance,
keep on pedalling and drinking
and one day maybe
I'll see the light.

Bandhavgarh

vultures soar above sal forest waiting for wafts of a kill

a chital tautens
a langur coughs
a predator space takes shape

presently
three tigers

Fences

1.

Three axe-women butterfly upstream
through a fence-hole into the forbidden.

A wild boar steps, stops, stares.

Which is more to fear here—
forest guards
or tigers, leopards, bears?

2.

Are we outside
like cattle
excluded from the leafy shade
looking in on wildlife
fenced for its own protection?

Or are we the ones in the cage
treading scorched earth
under lopped trees
trapped here
in the enclosure?

I Have My Yellow Boots On to Walk

after W. S. Graham

I have my yellow boots on to walk
down to the sea
the grey cloth ruffled and crumby
with little boats

I have my yellow boots on to sink
into the walking waters
submerge and find the world
just as it is

I have my yellow boots on to follow
in dead men's steps
to where the old engine
rusts at the shore

I have my yellow boots on to wander
out to where waves spume
gannets dive
fulmars soar

Under the Surface

stop

      move towards a moment
      when motion ceases;
      listen: a raven calls,
      leaves fall.

pause

      beside ripples, watch
      leaves gather into a flotilla
      with a mat of rushes
      ready for meditation.

invite

      share rushes, ripples, raven,
      leaves, come here
      into this day;
      to stand, staring into the water.

Walking

wonder:
> a river-wrack dance on incoming tide,
> two otters twining out to sea,
> moss under crushing footsteps,
> a radiant sedge,
> a raven overhead.

wondering:
> why one rowan toppled in the storm,
> upending boulders to survive
> all tangled, all-angled complexity,
> while the smaller simply
> shed another limb.

insight:
> mosses and lichens, liverworts and ferns
> will overgrow the wounded wood,
> scarred trunks will heal,
> the lightened crown will stand;
> there is elegance or there is sprawl.

coming back
> it is the same grey day
> but everything is different;
> even the river
> flows the other way.

Boats on the Kelvin

The flotilla was ship-built
on the Persian dry dock in the living room.
There were no rules—
we made it up as we went along.

Our white paper craft, like little flags,
we named for times; no mundane Mondays
or transient tomorrows, just absolutes:
always, never, soon, until, often, sometimes, now.

The launch was where the dark, sleek,
slate-clean river pauses
after the roaring weir,
before the bubbling bumps

beneath the Belmont bridge.
Corralled along a starting line
we set them free
to race to the eternity of sea.

Often capsized, until span,
now lost the chase to soon and sometimes.
Will never never conquer?
Does always always win?

The Falkland Burn

a babbled ballad from the bens
an ingle-ingle ootle-ootling thing

a symphony of plops and drips
all liquid linguistic fingerings

a long strong song
singing of mingling springs

Start at the Top

You don't need me to tell you how to get there, just go up from the bottom until you reach the cairn. Not the wood-henge. On a bit. Hurry up. You need to pant a bit on the way, it makes you feel good.

Ignore the roundhouse, it'll no doubt still be there in another four thousand years, and as Dr Johnson said, 'to go and see one bronze age hut is only to see that it is nothing, for there is neither art nor power in it, and seeing one is quite enough.'

Before you set off, look north, and fail to work out which one of the mountains is Ben Wyvis.

Carry a label in your pocket, but don't write *Ochralechia tartarea* on it, when it is pointed out to you, nor note its traditional use as a dye.

Of course you will need to carry a pencil in your pocket too.

When that memory of the old man Donnie, who had the allotment next to yours and complained about your weeds, is triggered by the cluster of coltsfoot flowers in sunshine, you can just forget it. There was a budding larch tree to hang the label on, but you missed it in your rush for the summit.

Have you started yet?

Cutting Peats

(for four voices, each reading simultaneously)

for Ray, Caroline and Anna

voice 1: cutting	voice 2: delivering	voice 3: laying out	voice 4: laying out
place the tusk			
stamp it down			
push forward	hold the peat		
back and up	pull it loose		
place the tusk	lift it up	bend and reach	
stamp it down	pass it out	take the peat	
push forward	hold the peat	stand and turn	
back and up	pull it loose	lug it back	
place the tusk	lift it up	lug it back	bend and reach
stamp it down	pass it out	lay it down	take the peat
push forward	hold the peat	walk to bank	stand and turn
back and up	pull it loose	walk to bank	lug it back
place the tusk	lift it up	bend and reach	lug it back
stamp it down	pass it out	take the peat	lay it down
push forward	hold the peat	stand and turn	run to bank
back and up	pull it loose	lug it back	take a breath
place the tusk	lift it up	lug it back	bend and reach
stamp it down	pass it out	lay it down	take the peat
push forward	hold the peat	walk to bank	stand and turn
back and up	pull it loose	walk to bank	lug it back
place the tusk	lift it up	bend and reach	lug it back
stamp it down	pass it out	take the peat	lay it down
stamp again	take a breath	stand and turn	run to bank
push forward	smell the peat	lug it back	take a breath
back and up	pull it loose	lug it back	watch the sky
place the tusk	lift it up	lay it down	bend and reach
stamp it down	pass it out	walk to bank	take the peat

slip a bit
say sorry
place the tusk
stamp it down
push forward
back and up
place the tusk
stamp it down
push forward
back and up
place the tusk
stamp it down
push forward
back and up

drop the peat
pick it up
say nae probs
pass it out
hold the peat
pull it loose
lift it up
pass it out
hold the peat
pull it loose
lift it up
pass it out
hold the peat
pull it loose
lift it up
pass it out

walk to bank
pause and laugh
bend and reach
take the peat
stand and turn
lug it back
lug it back
lay it down
walk to bank
walk to bank
bend and reach
take the peat
stand and turn
lug it back
lug it back
lay it down

stand and turn
lug it back
lug it back
lay it down
run to bank
take a breath
bend and reach
take the peat
stand and turn
lug it back
lug it back
lay it down
run to bank
take a breath
bend and reach
take the peat
stand and turn
lug it back
lug it back
lay it down

Take it Easy

Kneaded enough by time?
Sit somewhere warm,
allow yourself to rise.

Bask in the glow of now's fire
doing the nothing cats do.

Burn all stray scraps of must
(ought... should...).
See their tiny flames.

Attune

listen

stop your mouth
your mind
unwind

listen

take a breath
touch earth
berth

listen

hear the beats
hushed heart
fresh start

listen

be slow
let your soul
know whole

listen

this planet spins
rings
sings

listen

Green Bowl

I cannot put down the green bowl
its emptiness
shines

its lid
creates a space inside
where the future hides

Touch the Earth Gently

Touch the earth gently, knowing our lives
climax when we least expect them to.
Tickle the world like a child, feel it
tremble. It is vulnerable, like you,
wild, as you could be if you could only
abandon all wishes of security,
thrust aside ambition, learn today
love of the present. Treasure this moment,
burning with life, knowing you will one day be
limp; your skin cold, heart stopped,
lips silenced; internal organs,
juices and muscles hardening. Be soft,
aroused in all your senses, alert to now.
Finger the earth gently, and know.

Acknowledgements

I am very grateful to Sheila Wakefield for publishing, Elizabeth Rimmer for editing and Gerry Cambridge for designing and laying out this book.

Some of these poems would never have been written and the collection as a whole would have been very different were it not for the help and encouragement I received from Tom Leonard, my teacher and mentor, who sadly breathed his last breath shortly before publication. Thanks also to Chris Powici for his helpful and perceptive advice and to Maggie, John, Jorine, Romany, Anna, Becks and many others, far too numerous to name, who have helped me over the years by reading drafts or lending a listening ear to poems in progress.

Some of the poems have been published in literary magazines, anthologies or websites or listed in competitions, so I thank the editors and judges of all of the following for your support: Poetry Scotland, Northerly Gusts, Leeds International Poetry Competition, Dream Catcher, Stramash, Coffee House Poetry Competition, Ver Poetry Competition, Obsessed with Pipework, Cleave, The Rialto, New Writing Scotland, Scotia Extremis, Nature Writers, Like Leaves in Autumn, Surreal Poetry Competition, Buzzwords Competition, Northern Lights Competition, A Fresh Northerly, Brittle Star, Orbis, Northwords Now, Hidden City, Message in a Bottle, Acumen, Indian Ink, Poets' Republic, Scottish Poetry Library, StAnza Poetry Map, Gutter, Words in the Landscape, Pull of the Tide, Reforesting Scotland Journal, 14 Magazine.

Particular thanks to my Dad, my sister, all the Cohen clan and of course Bill, because poems don't happen without love.

'From the closest recesses of the human heart out into the wide wild world, these poems take us to where wolf bays, bear bathes, midges whine. Mandy Haggith's new collection is a lovely unmarked path that traverses continents, discovering peoples' sacred words for things, singing universal truths.'

—Kate Ashton

'In this fourth poetry collection, Why the Sky is Far Away, Mandy Haggith weaves poems seamlessly together as she explores the inter-connectedness of our lives with the physical environment. Her poems draw on her deep knowledge of the natural world and her empathy for life-forms beyond the human. The whole collection feels like a love song and celebration of home and habitat, a gentle reminder of our need for relationship with one another and with Planet Earth.'

—Christine De Luca

'These poems speak quietly of a natural world, loved and deeply understood. They are intimate with their subject matter, whether that be stories of indigenous people, family, travel, bears, tigers, swimming or simply planting seeds. They are beautifully crafted yet seem to live in the moment of their making, pitch perfect and wise—'rahayu'. A stunning collection to heighten the senses, and teach you how to look.'

—Chrys Salt

'[A collection] coherent with the consistency of theme in exploration of the wonders of the natural world. If this should sound 'worthy' then that's probably about the opposite of the feel of the book. It bristles and bustles with energy which somehow still pulses through the various and wonder-ful forms found for a strong series of celebrations.'

—Ian Stephen

A NOTE ON THE TYPES

This book is set in Seria Pro and Seria Sans Pro,
Dutch type designer Martin Majoor's graceful and distinctive
typefaces from 2000. Available in six and four weights
respectively, these versatile faces are suited
to a wide range of different uses including
the setting of poetry.